Contents

Landforms

The land is made of different shapes.
These shapes are called landforms.

Landforms

Islands

Cassie Mayer

www.heinemann.co.uk/library
Visit our website to find out more information about Heinemann Library books.

To order:
☎ Phone 44 (0) 1865 888066
  Send a fax to 44 (0) 1865 314091
📄 Visit the Heinemann Bookshop at www.heinemann.co.uk/library to browse our
💻 catalogue and order online.

First published in Great Britain by Heinemann Library,
Halley Court, Jordan Hill, Oxford OX2 8EJ, part of Harcourt
Education. Heinemann is a registered trademark of Harcourt
Education Ltd.

© Harcourt Education Ltd 2007
First published in paperback in 2007
The moral right of the proprietor has been asserted.

Editorial: Tracey Crawford, Cassie Mayer, Dan Nunn,
  and Sarah Chappelow
Design: Jo Hinton-Malivoire
Picture Research: Heather Mauldin and Tracy Cummins
Production: Duncan Gilbert

Originated by Chroma Graphics (Overseas) Pte. Ltd
Printed and bound in China by South China
Printing Company

ISBN 978 0 431 18233 9 (hardback)
11 10 09 08 07
10 9 8 7 6 5 4 3 2 1

ISBN 978 0 431 18356 5 (paperback)
12 11 10 09 08
10 9 8 7 6 5 4 3 2

British Library Cataloguing in Publication Data
Mayer, Cassie
  Islands. - (Landforms)
  1.Islands - Juvenile literature
  I.Title
  551.4'2

Acknowledgements
The publishers would like to thank the following for permission to
reproduce photographs: Corbis pp. 4 (river, Pat O'Hara; mountain,
Royalty Free; volcano, Galen Rowell; cave, Layne Kennedy),
5 (George Steinmetz), 9 (Yann Arthus-Bertrand), 10 (Richard
Hamilton Smith), 11 (Jonathan Blair), 12 (Craig Tuttle), 13 (Bob
Krist), 14 (Skyscan), 21 (Chris Lisle); Getty Images 7 (Haas), 8
(Herbert), 15 (Chesley), 16 (Josef Beck), 17 (John Lawrence), 18
(Art Wolfe), 19 (Suzanne & Nick Geary), 20 (Stewart Cohen), 23
(lighthouse, Lawrence; Bay of Plenty, Chesley).

Cover photograph of the island Culebra, Puerto Rico, reproduced
with permission of Corbis/Danny Lehman. Backcover image of
British Virgin Islands reproduced with permission of Getty Images/
Herbert.

Every effort has been made to contact copyright holders of any
material reproduced in this book. Any omissions will be rectified in
subsequent printings if notice is given to the publishers.

island

An island is a landform.
Islands are found all over the world.

What is an island?

An island is land with water all around it. Some islands are very big.

Some islands are very small.

Some islands are in seas and oceans.

Some islands are in rivers and lakes.

Some islands are close to each other.

When islands are close together it is called a chain.

Where are islands found?

Some islands are near the equator. These islands have hot weather all through the year.

Some islands are near the North or South Poles. These islands have very cold weather all through the year.

There are mountains under the seas and oceans. Some islands are formed by the tops of mountains under the water.

There are volcanoes under the seas and oceans too. Some islands are formed by the tops of volcanoes under the water.

Features of an island

Some islands have sandy beaches.

Some islands have high cliffs.

What lives on an island?

iguana

There are some islands where no plants or animals live. Other islands have lots of different plants and animals.

Some islands have plants, animals, and people!

Visiting islands

People like to visit islands.
Some people like to walk along
the cliff paths.

Some people like to enjoy
the quiet beaches and the
beautiful sea.

Island facts

Greenland is the largest island in the world. Most of the island is covered in ice.

The United Kingdom is the largest island in Europe. Over 60 million people live on this island.

Picture glossary

cliff rock that is very high and steep

volcano a mountain with a hole at the top

Index

Notes to parents and teachers

Before reading

Talk about islands. Explain that they are landforms which are surrounded by water. Some islands are big and many people live on them. Some islands are small and are uninhabited.

After reading

Look at an atlas or a globe. Help the children to find some islands. Find some that are near the equator and others that are near the North and South Poles.

Make an island by first making a mountain out of plasticine. Place it in the bottom of a washing up bowl or glass tank. Fill the bowl with water until only the peak of the mountain is above the water. You may like to add a few drops of blue colouring to the water. Talk about the land mass below the water and the island which is formed above the water. Encourage them to look at the mountain from above and from the sides.

The Island Dance: Tell three children to stand with their backs to each other and to hold hands. They are to be the island. Ask all the other children to form a circle around the "island". They should hold hands and gently move in towards the "island" and then out again, as waves lapping on the island shores. Play a CD of "ocean" music for the children to move to.